A Friend Called the Holy Spirit

MILDRED C. SCALES

WORKBOOK PRESS LLC
187 E Warm Springs Rd,
Suite B285, Las Vegas, NV 89119, USA

Website: https://workbookpress.com/
Hotline: 1-888-818-4856
Email: admin@workbookpress.com

Ordering Information:
Quantity sales. Special discounts are available on quantity purchases by corporations, associations, and others.
For details, contact the publisher at the address above.

Library of Congress Control Number:

ISBN-13:   000-0-000000-00-0 (Paperback Version)
              000-0-000000-00-0 (Digital Version)

REV. DATE: 10/06/2022

About the Author

Mildred C. Scales raised in a family of 15 children has been trained up to share, support, and protect those she love. Mother of one son and two daughters and wife of 48 years. Mildred has rarely worked outside of the home and for many years she has been a loving stay at home mother and wife.

If you were to ask her what is her profession by trade she would have a vast description of her responsibilities as a wife, mother, caregiver, teacher, defense attorney, taxi driver, chef, accountant, seamstress, counselor and prayer warrior...

Having a deep love for the Word of God Mildred attended the school of the Bible in Baltimore Maryland, and numerous other work shops and conferences, acquiring knowledge of God's Word.

Mildred Served as Prayer Ministry leader at her Church for eight years where she is considered a prayer warrior Leader, and a spiritual mother to a few women she holds dear to her heart. Mildred is a native of Baltimore, Maryland and is now rooted in Arlington, Texas.

I would like to thank God for this journal, for He has trusted me with His Word.

I thank my husband James Scales for his patience and respect for the ministry the Lord has assigned me to.

Thank you Pastor Dr. Michael Evans, Patricia Simon and, Veolia Myers for your encouragement.

Thanks to my daughter Monet Redd for her Patients and her computer skills.

Journal with The Holy Spirit Have a talk
with God

Enter into His gates with thanksgiving,
and into His courts with praise: Be
thankful unto Him, and bless his name. For
the LORD is good; his mercy is everlasting;
And His truth endures to all generations.

Worship the Lord from the depths of your
heart with pen and pencil.

Oh how we love You Lord, You are our
keeper, You are the shade upon our right
hand, thank You Heavenly Father, for Your
grace and for Your mercy.

This Journal is Dedicated to the memory of

My Parents Alease and Thomas Winkey And My Christian

Mother Beulah Johnson

"A Friend Called the Holy Spirit"

How did You do it Lord?

How did you know me so well?

If anyone had looked at me,

I'm certain they couldn't tell.

They couldn't see the loneliness.

I kept it deep inside.

But You looked into my spirit and You recognize the pride.

You kept tugging at my spirit, You

said child I know you well.

If only you would trust me,

I'll bless you more than you can tell.

So with a broken spirit,

I gave my will to You.

And You gave me a spiritual friend who

takes pleasure in serving You.

He told me that You loved me, You'll never leave my side.

And on my Christian journey, You sent Him for the ride.

Thank You Holy Spirit,

Mildred C. Scales

Fruit of
The Spirit

Love

Joy

Peace

Patience

Kindness

Goodness

Faith

Meekness

Self - control

Love

Love is patient, love is kind. It does
not envy, it does not boast, it is not proud.
It does not dishonor others,
it is not self-seeking, it is not easily
angered, it keeps no record of wrongs."

1 Corinthians 13:4-5 NIV

_____

_____

_____

_____

_____

_____

_____

_____

_____

_____

_____

_____

_____

_____

_____

_____

_____

_____

_____

_____

_____

"I love you, LORD; you are my strength."

Psalms 18:1 NL

_____

_____

_____

_____

_____

_____

_____

_____

_____

_____

_____

_____

_____

_____

_____

_____

_____

"Don't just pretend to love others. Really love them. Hate what is wrong.

Hold tightly to what is good."

Romans 12:9 NLT

_____

_____

_____

_____

_____

_____

_____

_____

_____

_____

_____

_____

_____

_____

_____

_____

_____

_____

_____

_____

_____

_____

"I love the LORD because he hears my voice and my prayer for mercy."

Psalms 116:1 NLT

_____

_____

_____

_____

_____

_____

_____

_____

_____

_____

_____

_____

_____

_____

_____

_____

_____

_____

_____

_____

"Beloved, if God so loved us, we ought also to love one another."

1 John 4:11 KJ

_____

_____

_____

_____

_____

_____

_____

_____

_____

_____

_____

_____

_____

_____

_____

_____

_____

_____

_____

_____

_____

_____

"Love is patient and kind. Love is not jealous or boastful or proud"

1 Corinthians 13:4 NLT

_____

_____

_____

_____

_____

_____

_____

_____

_____

_____

_____

_____

_____

_____

_____

_____

_____

_____

"In this the love of God was manifested toward us, that God has sent His only begotten Son into the world, that we might live through Him."

I John 4:9 NKJV

_____

_____

_____

_____

_____

_____

_____

_____

_____

_____

_____

_____

_____

_____

_____

_____

_____

_____

_____

"For God so loved the world that He gave His only begotten Son, that whoever believes in Him should not perish but have everlasting life."

John 3:16 NKJV

Heavenly father I thank You for loving me so much that You gave Your only Son that I might have Everlasting life.

Thank You for the gift.

Joy

"For his anger endureth but a moment; in his favour is life: weeping may endure for anight, but joy cometh in the morning."

Psalms 30:5 KJV

_____

_____

_____

_____

_____

_____

_____

_____

_____

_____

_____

_____

_____

_____

_____

_____

_____

_____

_____

"But let the godly rejoice. Let them be glad in God's presence. Let them be filled with joy."

Psalms 68:3 NLT

_____

_____

_____

_____

_____

_____

_____

_____

_____

_____

_____

_____

_____

_____

_____

_____

_____

_____

"Yet I will rejoice in the LORD, I will joy in the God of my salvation."

Habakkuk 3:18 NKJV

_____

_____

_____

_____

_____

_____

_____

_____

_____

_____

_____

_____

_____

_____

_____

_____

_____

_____

_____

_____

_____

_____

"My brethren, count it all joy when you fall into various trials, knowing that the testing of your faith produces patience."

James 1:2-3 NKJV

_____

_____

_____

_____

_____

_____

_____

_____

_____

_____

_____

_____

_____

_____

_____

_____

_____

_____

_____

_____

_____

"He brought out His people with joy, His chosen ones with gladness."

Psalms 105:43 NKJV

_____

_____

_____

_____

_____

_____

_____

_____

_____

_____

_____

_____

_____

_____

_____

_____

_____

_____

_____

_____

_____

"Those who sow in tears Shall reap in joy."

Psalms 126:5 NKJV

_____

_____

_____

_____

_____

_____

_____

_____

_____

_____

_____

_____

_____

_____

_____

_____

_____

_____

_____

_____

_____

_____

"You have made known to me the ways of life, You will make me full of joy in your presence."

Acts 2:28 NKJV

_____

_____

_____

_____

_____

_____

_____

_____

_____

_____

_____

_____

_____

_____

_____

_____

_____

_____

_____

_____

"For His anger is but for a moment, His favor is for life; Weeping may endure for a night, But joy comes in the morning."

Psalms 30:5 NKJV

*Father God Your joy is
my strength,
there is nothing I can't do
when I am in Your will.
thank you for Your
presence in my life.*

<u>Peace</u>

Peace I leave with you, my peace I give unto you: not as the world giveth, give I unto you. Let not your heart be troubled, neither let it be afraid.

John 14: 27 KJV

_____

_____

_____

_____

_____

_____

_____

_____

_____

_____

_____

_____

_____

_____

_____

_____

_____

_____

_____

_____

_____

"*Now the fruit of righteousness is sown in peace by those who make peace.*"

James 3:18 NKJV

_____

_____

_____

_____

_____

_____

_____

_____

_____

_____

_____

_____

_____

_____

_____

_____

_____

_____

_____

_____

""I create the fruit of the lips: Peace, peace to him who is far off and to him who is near," Says the LORD, "And I will heal him.""

Isaiah 57:19 NKJV

_____
_____
_____
_____
_____
_____
_____
_____
_____
_____
_____
_____
_____
_____
_____
_____
_____
_____
_____
_____
_____
_____

"casting all your care upon Him, for He cares for you."

I Peter 5:7 NKJV

_____

_____

_____

_____

_____

_____

_____

_____

_____

_____

_____

_____

_____

_____

_____

_____

_____

"Be careful for nothing; but in every thing by prayer and supplication with thanksgiving let your requests be made known unto God. And the peace of God, which passeth all understanding, shall keep your hearts and minds through Christ Jesus."

Philippians 4:6-KJV

_____

_____

_____

_____

_____

_____

_____

_____

_____

_____

_____

_____

_____

_____

_____

_____

_____

_____

"You will keep him in perfect peace, Whose mind is stayed on You, Because he trusts in You."

Isaiah 26:3 NKJV

_____

_____

_____

_____

_____

_____

_____

_____

_____

_____

_____

_____

_____

_____

_____

_____

_____

_____

"These things I have spoken to you, that in Me you may have peace. In the world you will have tribulation; but be of good cheer, I have overcome the world.""

John 16:33 NKJV

_____

_____

_____

_____

_____

_____

_____

_____

_____

_____

_____

_____

_____

_____

_____

_____

_____

_____

_____

_____

_____

"And the fruit of righteousness is sown in peace of them that make peace."

James 3:18 KJV

Father thank You for giving
me Your Son
who gives me Your peace,
which passes all
understanding
thank You for so much love.

Patience

We glory in tribulations also:

knowing that tribulation worketh

patience; And patience, experience;

and experience, hope:"

Roman 5:3-4 KJV

_____

_____

_____

_____

_____

_____

_____

_____

_____

_____

_____

_____

_____

_____

_____

_____

_____

_____

"For whatever things were written before were written for our learning, that we through the patience and comfort of the Scriptures might have hope."

Romans 15:4 NKJV

_____

_____

_____

_____

_____

_____

_____

_____

_____

_____

_____

_____

_____

_____

_____

_____

_____

_____

_____

_____

"Now may the God of patience and comfort grant you to be like-minded toward one another, according to Christ Jesus,"

Romans 15:5 NKJV

_____

_____

_____

_____

_____

_____

_____

_____

_____

_____

_____

_____

_____

_____

_____

_____

_____

_____

_____

"The end of a thing is better than its beginning; The patient in spirit is better than the proud in spirit."

Ecclesiastes 7:8 NKJV

_____

_____

_____

_____

_____

_____

_____

_____

_____

_____

_____

_____

_____

_____

_____

_____

_____

_____

_____

_____

_____

_____

"But let patience have its perfect work, that you may be perfect and complete, lacking nothing."

James 1:4 NKJV

_____

_____

_____

_____

_____

_____

_____

_____

_____

_____

_____

_____

_____

_____

_____

_____

_____

_____

_____

_____

_____

"strengthened with all might, according to His glorious power, for all patience and longsuffering with joy;"

Colossians 1:11 NKJV

_____

_____

_____

_____

_____

_____

_____

_____

_____

_____

_____

_____

_____

_____

_____

_____

_____

_____

_____

_____

"*My brethren, take the prophets, who spoke in the name of the Lord, as an example of suffering and patience.*"

James 5:10 NKJV

_____

_____

_____

_____

_____

_____

_____

_____

_____

_____

_____

_____

_____

_____

_____

_____

_____

"The end of a thing is better than its beginning; The patient in spirit is better than the proud in spirit."

Ecclesiastes 7:8 NKJV

Heavenly Father thank
You for your patience with
me as You Mold me
into who You have
ordained me to be.
You are an awesome God.

Kindness

"And be ye kind one to another,

tenderhearted, forgiving one another,

even as God for Christ's

sake hath forgiven you."

Ephesians 4:32 KJV

_____

_____

_____

_____

_____

_____

_____

_____

_____

_____

_____

_____

_____

_____

_____

_____

_____

_____

"to speak evil of no one, to be peaceable, gentle, showing all humility to all men."

Titus 3:2 NKJV

_____

_____

_____

_____

_____

_____

_____

_____

_____

_____

_____

_____

_____

_____

_____

_____

_____

"But the wisdom that is from above is first pure, then peaceable, gentle, willing to yield, full of mercy and good fruits, without partiality and without hypocrisy."

James 3:17 NKJV

_____

_____

_____

_____

_____

_____

_____

_____

_____

_____

_____

_____

_____

_____

_____

_____

_____

_____

_____

_____

_____

"For His merciful kindness is great toward us, And the truth of the LORD endures forever. Praise the LORD!"

Psalms 117:2 NKJV

_____

_____

_____

_____

_____

_____

_____

_____

_____

_____

_____

_____

_____

_____

_____

_____

_____

_____

_____

_____

_____

"Therefore, as the elect of God, holy and beloved, put on tender mercies, kindness, humility, meekness, longsuffering;"

Colossians 3:12 NKJV

_____

_____

_____

_____

_____

_____

_____

_____

_____

_____

_____

_____

_____

_____

_____

_____

_____

_____

"by purity, by knowledge, by longsuffering, by kindness, by the Holy Spirit, by sincere love,"

II Corinthians 6:6 NKJV

_____

_____

_____

_____

_____

_____

_____

_____

_____

_____

_____

_____

_____

_____

_____

_____

_____

_____

_____

"But the fruit of the Spirit is love, joy, peace, longsuffering, kindness, goodness, faithfulness,"

Galatians 5:22 NKJV

_____

_____

_____

_____

_____

_____

_____

_____

_____

_____

_____

_____

_____

_____

_____

_____

"But love your enemies, do good, and lend, hoping for nothing in return; and your reward will be great, and you will be sons of the Most High. For He is kind to the unthankful and evil."

Luke 6:35 NKJV

My king and my God Your
Loving kindness is too much
for me to Understand
I have not deserved
all of Your kindness towards
me. I give you Praise.

Goodness

"Surely goodness and mercy shall follow me all the days of my life: and I will dwell in the house of the Lord for ever." Psalms 23:6 KJV

_____

_____

_____

_____

_____

_____

_____

_____

_____

_____

_____

_____

_____

_____

_____

_____

_____

_____

_____

_____

_____

_____

_____

_____

"Oh, that men would give thanks to the LORD for His goodness, And for His wonderful works to the children of men!"

Psalms 107:8 NKJV

_____

_____

_____

_____

_____

_____

_____

_____

_____

_____

_____

_____

_____

_____

_____

"Oh, how great is Your goodness, Which You have laid up for those who fear You, Which You have prepared for those who trust in You In the presence of the sons of men!"

Psalms 31:19 NKJV

_____

_____

_____

_____

_____

_____

_____

_____

_____

_____

_____

_____

_____

_____

_____

_____

_____

_____

"Blessed is the man You choose, And cause to approach You, That he may dwell in Your courts. We shall be satisfied with the goodness of Your house, Of Your holy temple."

Psalms 65:4 NKJV

_____

_____

_____

_____

_____

_____

_____

_____

_____

_____

_____

_____

_____

_____

_____

_____

_____

_____

_____

_____

_____

"So you may walk in the way of goodness, And keep to the paths of righteousness."

Proverbs 2:20 NKJV

_____

_____

_____

_____

_____

_____

_____

_____

_____

_____

_____

_____

_____

_____

_____

_____

_____

_____

_____

_____

_____

"For He satisfies the longing soul, And fills the hungry soul with goodness."

Psalms 107:9 NKJV

_____

_____

_____

_____

_____

_____

_____

_____

_____

_____

_____

_____

_____

_____

_____

_____

_____

_____

_____

"He loves righteousness and justice; The earth is full of the goodness of the LORD."

Psalms 33:5 NKJV

_____

_____

_____

_____

_____

_____

_____

_____

_____

_____

_____

_____

_____

_____

_____

_____

_____

_____

_____

_____

"Oh, that men would give thanks to the LORD for His goodness,
And for His wonderful works to the children of men!"

Psalms 107:8 NKJV

Heavenly father Your goodness and Your mercy follows me all the Days of my life and I will dwell in Your presence forever thank You for the privilege.

Faith

"Faith is the confidence that what we hope for will actually happen; it gives us assurance about things we cannot see."

Hebrews 11:1 NLT

_____

_____

_____

_____

_____

_____

_____

_____

_____

_____

_____

_____

_____

_____

_____

_____

_____

_____

_____

_____

_____

_____

"For we walk by faith, not by sight."

II Corinthians 5:7 NKJV

_____
_____
_____
_____
_____
_____
_____
_____
_____
_____
_____
_____
_____
_____
_____
_____
_____
_____
_____
_____

"But He said to them, "Why are you so fearful? How is it that you have no faith?""

Mark 4:40 NKJV

_____
_____
_____
_____
_____
_____
_____
_____
_____
_____
_____
_____
_____
_____
_____
_____
_____
_____
_____
_____
_____
_____

"Thus also faith by itself, if it does not have works, is dead."

James 2:17 NKJV

_____
_____
_____
_____
_____
_____
_____
_____
_____
_____
_____
_____
_____
_____
_____
_____
_____
_____
_____

"Watch, stand fast in the faith, be brave, be strong."

I Corinthians 16:13 NKJV

_____

_____

_____

_____

_____

_____

_____

_____

_____

_____

_____

_____

_____

_____

_____

_____

_____

_____

_____

_____

_____

"For you are all sons of God through faith in Christ Jesus."

Galatians 3:26 NKJV

_____

_____

_____

_____

_____

_____

_____

_____

_____

_____

_____

_____

_____

_____

_____

_____

_____

_____

_____

_____

"Now faith is the substance of things hoped for, the evidence of things not seen."

Hebrews 11:1 NKJV

_____

_____

_____

_____

_____

_____

_____

_____

_____

_____

_____

_____

_____

_____

_____

_____

"But without faith it is impossible to please Him, for he who comes to God must believe that He is, and that He is a rewarder of those who diligently seek Him."

Hebrews 11:6 NKJV

Father I know without faith
it is impossible to please You,
help me with my unbelief so
that
I can grow from little
faith to great faith.
All You require is
mustered seed faith.
Thank You for knowing me,
and for Your mercies that are
new every morning.
Great is Your faithfulness.

Meekness

But the wisdom that is from above

is first pure, then peaceable, gentle,

and easy to be entreated, full of

mercy and good fruits, without

partiality, and without hypocrisy."

James 3:17 KJV

_____

_____

_____

_____

_____

_____

_____

_____

_____

_____

_____

_____

_____

_____

_____

_____

_____

_____

_____

"Who is wise and understanding among you? Let him show by good conduct that his works are done in the meekness of wisdom."

James 3:13 NKJV

_____

_____

_____

_____

_____

_____

_____

_____

_____

_____

_____

_____

_____

_____

_____

_____

_____

_____

_____

_____

_____

"Repay no one evil for evil. Have regard for good things in the sight of all men."

Romans 12:17 NKJV

_____

_____

_____

_____

_____

_____

_____

_____

_____

_____

_____

_____

_____

_____

_____

_____

_____

_____

_____

_____

"He leads the humble in doing right, teaching them his way."

Psalms 25:9 NLT

_____

_____

_____

_____

_____

_____

_____

_____

_____

_____

_____

_____

_____

_____

_____

_____

_____

_____

"(Now Moses was very humble—more humble than any other person on earth.)"

Numbers 12:3 NLT

_____

_____

_____

_____

_____

_____

_____

_____

_____

_____

_____

_____

_____

_____

_____

_____

_____

_____

_____

"Put away your sword," Jesus told him. "Those who use the sword will die by the sword."

Matthew 26:52 NLT

_____

_____

_____

_____

_____

_____

_____

_____

_____

_____

_____

_____

_____

_____

_____

_____

_____

_____

"The lowly will possess the land and will live in peace and prosperity."

Psalms 37:11 NLT

_____

_____

_____

_____

_____

_____

_____

_____

_____

_____

_____

_____

_____

_____

_____

_____

_____

_____

_____

_____

_____

"They must not slander anyone and must avoid quarreling. Instead, they should be gentle and show true humility to everyone."

Titus 3:2 NLT

Father you said in Your Word
the meek shall inherit the earth,
help me To be in control
over the power
You have given me, and to
submit to Your Divine Will
without any complaints.

Self control

"So I tell you this, and insist

on it in the Lord, that you

must no longer live

as the Gentiles do, in the futility

of their thinking."

Ephesians 4:17 NIV

_____

_____

_____

_____

_____

_____

_____

_____

_____

_____

_____

_____

_____

_____

_____

_____

_____

_____

_____

"He who is slow to anger is better than the mighty, And he who rules his spirit than he who takes a city."

Proverbs 16:32 NKJV

_____

_____

_____

_____

_____

_____

_____

_____

_____

_____

_____

_____

_____

_____

_____

_____

_____

_____

_____

"Don't you realize that your body is the temple of the Holy Spirit, who lives in you and was given to you by God? You do not belong to yourself,"

1 Corinthians 6:19 NLT

_____

_____

_____

_____

_____

_____

_____

_____

_____

_____

_____

_____

_____

_____

_____

_____

_____

_____

_____

_____

_____

_____

_____

"*A person without self-control is like a city with broken-down walls.*"

Proverbs 25:28 NLT

_____

_____

_____

_____

_____

_____

_____

_____

_____

_____

_____

_____

_____

_____

_____

_____

_____

_____

_____

_____

_____

"Better to be patient than powerful; better to have self-control than to conquer a city."

Proverbs 16:32 NLT

_____

_____

_____

_____

_____

_____

_____

_____

_____

_____

_____

_____

_____

_____

_____

_____

_____

_____

_____

_____

"But when the leading priests and the elders made their accusations against him, Jesus remained silent."

Matthew 27:12 NLT

_____

_____

_____

_____

_____

_____

_____

_____

_____

_____

_____

_____

_____

_____

_____

_____

_____

_____

_____

"But the end of all things is at hand: be ye therefore sober, and watch unto prayer."

1 Peter 4:7 KJV

_____

_____

_____

_____

_____

_____

_____

_____

_____

_____

_____

_____

_____

_____

_____

_____

_____

_____

_____

_____

_____

_____

_____

_____

"Do not waste time arguing over godless ideas and old wives' tales. Instead, train yourself to be godly."

1 Timothy 4:7 NLT

Father it is so important to me to represent You well in this earth, help me to have good behavior in difficult situations, to be concerned of others feelings, and to remember that this journey is not about me, but about Your will to be done on earth as it is in heaven.

Love

Joy

Peace

Patience

Kindness

Goodness

Faith

Meekness

_____

_____

_____

_____

_____

_____

_____

_____

_____

_____

_____

_____

_____

_____

_____

_____

_____

_____

_____

Self control

A Prayer of Thanksgiving

I waited patiently for the Lord and He inclined unto me and heard my cry. He brought me up also out of a horrible pit, out of the Miry clay and set my feet upon a rock and established my going, then said I Lo I come in the volume of the book it is written of me I delight to do Thy will, o my God Thy law is within my heart

My King and my God, my Lord and my Savior, the Bishop of my soul. I come in the name of Jesus, thanking You and blessing You this morning just for who You are, thank You for assured prayer, thank You for being my help, my joy, my peace, my comfort, for being a healer, a deliverer, a friend that sticks closer than a brother. Father I bless Your name. Forgive me for anything that I have done that is not pleasing in your sight. Bless those that have wronged me, and drawn them close to you teach them your ways so that you can use them for your Honor, and your glory. Father bless my family and friends and this Nation and World cover them in your blood, build a hedge of protection around them protect them from all hurt harm and danger. Thank you for being our keeper, for being the shade upon our right hand, thank you that you neither sleep nor slumber, thank you for the plans you have for me, plans of peace and not of evil to give me hope, thank you for leaving your Holy Spirit with me. He is a comforter, a teacher, a friend and I am so grateful that he lives inside of me for you have made our bodies the temple of your Holy Spirit, Father thank you, I praise you honor and bless your name.

In Jesus Name I pray Amen

_____

_____

_____

_____

_____

_____

_____

_____

_____

_____

_____

_____

_____

_____

_____

_____

_____

_____

_____

"I will praise the name of God with a song, and will magnify him with thanksgiving."

Psalms 69:30 KJV

"Let us come before his presence with thanksgiving, and make a joyful noise unto him with psalms."

Psalms 95:2 KJV

_____

_____

_____

_____

_____

_____

_____

_____

_____

_____

_____

_____

_____

_____

_____

_____

_____

_____

"Enter into his gates with thanksgiving, and into his courts with praise: be thankful unto him, and bless his name."

Psalms 100:4 KJV

_____

_____

_____

_____

_____

_____

_____

_____

_____

_____

_____

_____

_____

_____

_____

_____

_____

_____

_____

_____

_____

_____

"Continue in prayer, and watch in the same with thanksgiving;"

Colossians 4:2 KJV

_____

_____

_____

_____

_____

_____

_____

_____

_____

_____

_____

_____

_____

_____

_____

_____

_____

_____

_____

_____

"But I will sacrifice unto thee with the voice of thanksgiving; I will pay that that I have vowed. Salvation is of the Lord."

Jonah 2:9 KJV

_____

_____

_____

_____

_____

_____

_____

_____

_____

_____

_____

_____

_____

_____

_____

_____

_____

_____

_____

_____

_____

_____

"Be careful for nothing; but in every thing by prayer and supplication with thanksgiving let your requests be made known unto God."

Philippians 4:6 KJV

_____

_____

_____

_____

_____

_____

_____

_____

_____

_____

_____

_____

_____

_____

_____

_____

_____

_____

_____

_____

"That I may publish with the voice of thanksgiving, and tell of all thy wondrous works."

Psalms 26:7 KJV

_____

_____

_____

_____

_____

_____

_____

_____

_____

_____

_____

_____

_____

_____

_____

_____

_____

_____

_____

_____

"*Saying, Amen: Blessing, and glory, and wisdom, and thanksgiving, and honour, and power, and might, be unto our God for ever and ever. Amen.*"

Revelation 7:12 KJV

When Praying Gods Protection

If I take the wings of the morning and dwell in the uttermost parts of the sea, even there your hand shall lead me and your right hand shall hold me.

My Lord and my savior my King and my God creator of all good and perfect things, I come in the name of Jesus thanking you for your presence in my life for knowing me, for knowing my thoughts afar off, for being acquainted with all my ways, Lord such knowledge is too wonderful for me too great for me to know. I could never escape from your spirit neither get away from your presence. If I go up to heaven you are there, if I go down to hell you are there even at the farthest limits of the Sea you will lead me and hold me. Thank you Father for never leaving me nor forsaking me. Your Word says that I am fearfully and wonderfully made my soul knows well that your works are marvelous, thank you Father that your thoughts of me are more in number than the sands of the sea. Father search my heart try me and know my thoughts Point out anything in me that offends you and lead me along the path of everlasting life

In Jesus Name I pray Amen

_____

_____

_____

_____

_____

_____

_____

_____

_____

_____

_____

_____

_____

_____

_____

_____

_____

_____

"The Lord shall preserve thy going out and thy coming in from this time forth, and even for evermore."

Psalms 121:8 KJV

_____

_____

_____

_____

_____

_____

_____

_____

_____

_____

_____

_____

_____

_____

_____

_____

_____

_____

_____

_____

_____

_____

"The Lord also will be a refuge for the oppressed, a refuge in times of trouble."

Psalms 9:9 KJV

_____

_____

_____

_____

_____

_____

_____

_____

_____

_____

_____

_____

_____

_____

_____

_____

_____

_____

_____

_____

"I laid me down and slept; I awaked; for the Lord sustained me."

Psalms 3:5 KJV

_____

_____

_____

_____

_____

_____

_____

_____

_____

_____

_____

_____

_____

_____

_____

_____

_____

_____

_____

_____

"Hold up my goings in thy paths, that my footsteps slip not."

Psalms 17:5 KJV

_____
_____
_____
_____
_____
_____
_____
_____
_____
_____
_____
_____
_____
_____
_____
_____

"Though I walk in the midst of trouble, You will revive me; You will stretch out Your hand Against the wrath of my enemies, And Your right hand will save me."

Psalms 138:7 NKJV

_____

_____

_____

_____

_____

_____

_____

_____

_____

_____

_____

_____

_____

_____

_____

_____

_____

_____

_____

_____

_____

"Though he fall, he shall not be utterly cast down: for the Lord upholdeth him with his hand."

Psalms 37:24 KJV

_____

_____

_____

_____

_____

_____

_____

_____

_____

_____

_____

_____

_____

_____

_____

_____

_____

"But I will sing of thy power; yea, I will sing aloud of thy mercy in the morning: for thou hast been my defence and refuge in the day of my trouble."

Psalms 59:16 KJV

Prayer of Trust

In the Lord I put my trust; how can you say to me to my soul flee as a bird to your mountain? If the foundations are destroyed what can the righteous do? The LORD is in his holy temple The LORD's throne is in heaven; His eyelids test the sons of men. My King and my God, my Lord and my savior, I come in the name of Jesus thanking you for your mercies that are new every morning, great is your faithfulness. Father I ask you to forgive me for anything that I have thought, said, or done, that is not pleasing in your sight. Thank you for morning prayer. The Psalmist said in your word, My voice shalt thou here in the morning in the morning will I direct my prayer unto you and will look up. Thank you Father that the prayers of a righteous man availeth much. Father be with me this day lead me in a plane path make your will so clear to me that I will have no question that it is you directing my life, I am so blessed to be used by you. You are a shield for me my glory and the lifter of my head, and God have I put my trust: I will not be afraid of what man can do unto me.

In Jesus Name I pray Amen

_____

_____

_____

_____

_____

_____

_____

_____

_____

_____

_____

_____

_____

_____

_____

_____

_____

"In God have I put my trust: I will not be afraid what man can do unto me."

Psalms 56:11 KJV

_____

_____

_____

_____

_____

_____

_____

_____

_____

_____

_____

_____

_____

_____

_____

_____

_____

_____

"In the Lord put I my trust: how say ye to my soul, Flee as a bird to your mountain?"

Psalms 11:1 KJV

_____

_____

_____

_____

_____

_____

_____

_____

_____

_____

_____

_____

_____

_____

_____

_____

_____

_____

_____

"And the Lord shall help them, and deliver them: he shall deliver them from the wicked, and save them, because they trust in him."

Psalms 37:40 KJV

_____

_____

_____

_____

_____

_____

_____

_____

_____

_____

_____

_____

_____

_____

_____

_____

_____

_____

"It is better to trust in the Lord than to put confidence in princes."

Psalms 118:9 KJV

_____

_____

_____

_____

_____

_____

_____

_____

_____

_____

_____

_____

_____

_____

_____

_____

_____

_____

"*Trust in him at all times; ye people, pour out your heart before him: God is a refuge for us.*

Psalms 62:8 KJV

_____
_____
_____
_____
_____
_____
_____
_____
_____
_____
_____
_____
_____
_____
_____
_____
_____
_____

"Offer the sacrifices of righteousness, and put your trust in the Lord."

Psalms 4:5 KJV

_____

_____

_____

_____

_____

_____

_____

_____

_____

_____

_____

_____

_____

_____

_____

_____

_____

"I will both lay me down in peace, and sleep: for thou, Lord, only makest me dwell in safety."

Psalms 4:8 KJV

Comfort in The LORD

"I will bless the Lord at all times: his praise shall continually be in my mouth. My soul shall make her boast in the Lord: the humble shall hear there of, and be glad. O magnify the Lord with me, and let us exalt his name together. I sought the Lord, and he heard me, and delivered me from all my fears. Oh taste and see that the Lord is good: blessed is the man that trsuteth in him. Many are the afflictions of the righteous: but the Lord delivereth him out of them all." Father in the name of Jesus I come into your presence thanking you for another day, and thanking you for your provision. You have supplied all of my needs, you have given me health and strength, your peace that passes all under-standing. And I give you praise just for who you are. Thank you for being true to your Word. A God that I can trust a God that will never leave me nor forsake me, thank you for your Word that keeps me. You said not to worry about anything but to pray about everything with thanksgiving. Then we will experience your peace, and your peace will guard our heart and mind as we live in Christ Jesus. Father I love you and I bless your name.

In Jesus Name I pray Amen

_____

_____

_____

_____

_____

_____

_____

_____

_____

_____

_____

_____

_____

_____

_____

_____

_____

_____

"Yea, though I walk through the valley of the shadow of death, I will fear no evil: for thou art with me; thy rod and thy staff they comfort me."

Psalms 23:4 KJV

_____

_____

_____

_____

_____

_____

_____

_____

_____

_____

_____

_____

_____

_____

_____

_____

_____

"Who comforteth us in all our tribulation, that we may be able to comfort them which are in any trouble, by the comfort wherewith we ourselves are comforted of God."

2 Corinthians 1:4 KJV

_____

_____

_____

_____

_____

_____

_____

_____

_____

_____

_____

_____

_____

_____

_____

_____

_____

_____

_____

_____

"Now we exhort you, brethren, warn them that are unruly, comfort the feebleminded, support the weak, be patient toward all men."

1 Thessalonians 5:14 KJV

_____

_____

_____

_____

_____

_____

_____

_____

_____

_____

_____

_____

_____

_____

_____

_____

_____

_____

_____

"Let, I pray thee, thy merciful kindness be for my comfort, according to thy word unto thy servant."

Psalms 119:76 KJV

_____

_____

_____

_____

_____

_____

_____

_____

_____

_____

_____

_____

_____

_____

_____

_____

_____

_____

_____

_____

_____

_____

"Finally, brethren, farewell. Be perfect, be of good comfort, be of one mind, live in peace; and the God of love and peace shall be with you."

2 Corinthians 13:11 KJV

_____

_____

_____

_____

_____

_____

_____

_____

_____

_____

_____

_____

_____

_____

_____

_____

_____

"Blessed be God, even the Father of our Lord Jesus Christ, the Father of mercies, and the God of all comfort;"

2 Corinthians 1:3 KJV

_____

_____

_____

_____

_____

_____

_____

_____

_____

_____

_____

_____

_____

_____

_____

_____

_____

_____

"Yea, though I walk through the valley of the shadow of death, I will fear no evil: for thou art with me; thy rod and thy staff they comfort me."

Psalms 23:4 KJV

The Holy Spirit is God

Acts 5:3, 4

The Holy Spirit of God is a Person, as much as The Father and Son are persons, And therefore experiences all the sinless elements involved within a divine personality.

He has a mind (Rom. 8:27)

He searches out the human mind.

(Isaiah 64:4)

He has a will. (1 Cor. 12:11)

He forbids. (Acts 16:6,7)

He permits. (Acts 16:10)

He speaks. (Acts 8:29)

He love's (Rom. 15:30)

He grieves. (Eph. 4:30)

He prays. Rom. 8:26)

_____

_____

_____

_____

_____

_____

_____

_____

_____

_____

_____

_____

_____

_____

_____

_____

_____

_____

"But when the Father sends the Advocate as my representative—that is, the Holy Spirit—he will teach you everything and will remind you of everything I have told you."

John 14:26 NLT

_____

_____

_____

_____

_____

_____

_____

_____

_____

_____

_____

_____

_____

_____

_____

_____

_____

"Even as Peter was saying these things, the Holy Spirit fell upon all who were listening to the message."

Acts of the Apostles 10:44 NLT

"Do not stifle the Holy Spirit."

1 Thessalonians 5:19 NLT

_____

_____

_____

_____

_____

_____

_____

_____

_____

_____

_____

_____

_____

_____

_____

_____

_____

_____

_____

_____

_____

"Then Peter and John laid their hands upon these believers, and they received the Holy Spirit."

Acts of the Apostles 8:17 NLT

_____

_____

_____

_____

_____

_____

_____

_____

_____

_____

_____

_____

_____

_____

_____

_____

_____

_____

_____

_____

"Did you receive the Holy Spirit when you believed?" he asked them. "No," they replied, "we haven't even heard that there is a Holy Spirit.""

Acts of the Apostles 19:2 NLT

"Then he breathed on them and said, "Receive the Holy Spirit."

John 20:22 NLT

" "John baptized with water, but in just a few days you will be baptized with the Holy Spirit.""

Acts of the Apostles 1:5 NLT

_____

_____

_____

_____

_____

_____

_____

_____

_____

_____

_____

_____

_____

_____

_____

_____

_____

Jesus answered, Verily, verily, I say unto thee, Except a man be born of water and of the spirit, he cannot enter into the kingdom of God.

John 3:5 KJV

"And God confirmed the message by giving signs and wonders and various miracles and gifts of the Holy Spirit whenever he chose."

Hebrews 2:4 NLT

_____

_____

_____

_____

_____

_____

_____

_____

_____

_____

_____

_____

_____

_____

_____

_____

_____

_____

"I didn't know he was the one, but when God sent me to baptize with water, he told me, 'The one on whom you see the Spirit descend and rest is the one who will baptize with the Holy Spirit.'"

John 1:33 NLT

_____

_____

_____

_____

_____

_____

_____

_____

_____

_____

_____

_____

_____

_____

_____

_____

_____

_____

_____

_____

_____

"For by that one offering he forever made perfect those who are being made holy. And the Holy Spirit also testifies that this is so. For he says,"

Hebrews 10:14-15 NLT

_____

_____

_____

_____

_____

_____

_____

_____

_____

_____

_____

_____

_____

_____

_____

_____

_____

_____

_____

_____

_____

"And my message and my preaching were very plain. Rather than using clever and persuasive speeches, I relied only on the power of the Holy Spirit."

1 Corinthians 2:4 NLT

_____

_____

_____

_____

_____

_____

_____

_____

_____

_____

_____

_____

_____

_____

_____

_____

_____

_____

_____

_____

_____

_____

""Then John testified, "I saw the Holy Spirit descending like a dove from heaven and resting upon him." "

John 1:32 NLT

_____

_____

_____

_____

_____

_____

_____

_____

_____

_____

_____

_____

_____

_____

_____

_____

_____

""And when you are brought to trial in the synagogues and before rulers and authorities, don't worry about how to defend yourself or what to say, for the Holy Spirit will teach you at that time what needs to be said.""

Luke 12:11-12 NLT

_____

_____

_____

_____

_____

_____

_____

_____

_____

_____

_____

_____

_____

_____

_____

_____

_____

_____

""And now I will send the Holy Spirit, just as my Father promised. But stay here in the city until the Holy Spirit comes and fills you with power from heaven.""

Luke 24:49 NLT

_____

_____

_____

_____

_____

_____

_____

_____

_____

_____

_____

_____

_____

_____

_____

_____

_____

_____

"The Holy Spirit said to Philip, "Go over and walk along beside the carriage." Philip ran over and heard the man reading from the prophet Isaiah. Philip asked, "Do you understand what you are reading?""

Acts of the Apostles 8:29-30 NLT

_____

_____

_____

_____

_____

_____

_____

_____

_____

_____

_____

_____

_____

_____

_____

_____

_____

_____

"and he has identified us as his own by placing the Holy Spirit in our hearts as the first installment that guarantees everything he has promised us."

2 Corinthians 1:22 NLT

_____

_____

_____

_____

_____

_____

_____

_____

_____

_____

_____

_____

_____

_____

_____

_____

_____

_____

_____

_____

_____

_____

"We are witnesses of these things and so is the Holy Spirit, who is given by God to those who obey him.""

Acts of the Apostles 5:32 NLT

_____

_____

_____

_____

_____

_____

_____

_____

_____

_____

_____

_____

_____

_____

_____

_____

_____

_____

"God, who knows the heart, showed that he accepted them by giving the Holy Spirit to them, just as he did to us."

Acts 15:8 NIV

_____

_____

_____

_____

_____

_____

_____

_____

_____

_____

_____

_____

_____

_____

_____

_____

"Hold on to the pattern of wholesome teaching you learned from me—a pattern shaped by the faith and love that you have in Christ Jesus. Through the power of the Holy Spirit who lives within us, carefully guard the precious truth that has been entrusted to you."

2 Timothy 1:13-14 NLT

_____

_____

_____

_____

_____

_____

_____

_____

_____

_____

_____

_____

_____

_____

_____

_____

_____

"Humans can reproduce only human life, but the Holy Spirit gives birth to spiritual life."

John 3:6 NLT

_____

_____

_____

_____

_____

_____

_____

_____

_____

_____

_____

_____

_____

_____

_____

_____

_____

_____

_____

_____

_____

"So if you sinful people know how to give good gifts to your children, how much more will your heavenly Father give the Holy Spirit to those who ask him.""

Luke 11:13 NLT

_____

_____

_____

_____

_____

_____

_____

_____

_____

_____

_____

_____

_____

_____

_____

_____

_____

_____

"So I tell you, every sin and blasphemy can be forgiven—except blasphemy against the Holy Spirit, which will never be forgiven."

Matthew 12:31 NLT

_____

_____

_____

_____

_____

_____

_____

_____

_____

_____

_____

_____

_____

_____

_____

_____

"Then Peter said, "Ananias, why have you let Satan fill your heart? You lied to the Holy Spirit, and you kept some of the money for yourself. The property was yours to sell or not sell, as you wished. And after selling it, the money was also yours to give away. How could you do a thing like this? You weren't lying to us but to God!""

Acts of the Apostles 5:3-4 NLT

_____

_____

_____

_____

_____

_____

_____

_____

_____

_____

_____

_____

_____

_____

_____

_____

_____

_____

_____

_____

_____

_____

"and the Holy Spirit, in bodily form, descended on him like a dove. And a voice from heaven said, "You are my dearly loved Son, and you bring me great joy. ""

Luke 3:22 NLT

_____

_____

_____

_____

_____

_____

_____

_____

_____

_____

_____

_____

_____

_____

_____

_____

_____

_____

_____

_____

_____

_____

"Then when Paul laid his hands on them, the Holy Spirit came on them, and they spoke in other tongues and prophesied."

Acts of the Apostles 19:6 NLT

_____

_____

_____

_____

_____

_____

_____

_____

_____

_____

_____

_____

_____

_____

_____

_____

_____

_____

_____

"That is why the Holy Spirit says, "Today when you hear his voice, don't harden your hearts as Israel did when they rebelled, when they tested me in the wilderness."

Hebrews 3:7-8 NLT

_____

_____

_____

_____

_____

_____

_____

_____

_____

_____

_____

_____

_____

_____

_____

_____

_____

"Don't be drunk with wine, because that will ruin your life. Instead, be filled with the Holy Spirit,"

Ephesians 5:18 NLT

_____

_____

_____

_____

_____

_____

_____

_____

_____

_____

_____

_____

_____

_____

_____

_____

_____

_____

"But the Holy Spirit produces this kind of fruit in our lives: love, joy, peace, patience, kindness, goodness, faithfulness, gentleness, and self-control. There is no law against these things!"

Galatians 5:22-23 NLT

Hungry for God

"As the deer pants for the water brooks, So pants my soul for You, O God. My soul thirsts for God, for the living God. When shall I come and appear before God?" Deep calls unto deep. Psalms 42:1-2, 7 NKJV Father in the name of Jesus I come before your throne thanking you For your everlasting, unconditional love for me, and for your precious Holy Spirit that comforts me, and brings your word into my remembrance. There are not words to describe your Greatness Your power, your Faithfulness and your creation, you are all Knowing, ever present, all powerful, unchangeable God, there is No God Greater then you. I honor your name you are worthy to be praised. Thank you for your mercies that are new every morning, for your keeping power you are my only place of safety, In you do I put my trust. "Thou wilt show me the path of life: in thy presence is fullness of joy; at thy right hand there are pleasures for evermore." Psalms 16:11 KJV What is man that you are mindful of us. You have made our bodies the Temple of the Holy Spirit. The Kingdom of God is within us. You have put all things under our feet, and giving us dominion over your creation. You keep us clothed in our right Minds, you give us protection, and you provide for us you supply all of our needs According to your riches in Glory, you are an Awesome God and you alone are worthy to be Praised.

In Jesus Name I pray Amen

Love

Joy

Peace

Patience

Kindness

Goodness

Faith

Meekness

Self control

Love

Joy

Peace

Patience

Kindness

Goodness

Faith

Meekness

Self control

Love

Joy

Peace

Patience

Kindness

Goodness

Faith

Meekness

Self control

Word from the Author

"We can make plans, however, the LORD determines our steps. Life is a mystery. We make plans of how, and what our life will be like, but who knows what tomorrow will bring. God has a plan for each of our lives, and they are plans of good and not evil to give us hope, Every trial every tribulation is to teach us how to live a more fruitful life. One thing we can count on is that He is with us no matter how dark it may seem. Enjoy your mountain top experiences and know that you are not alone in the valley of life. We serve an awesome God and you can trust in Him. "Even when we walk through the darkest valley, we don't have to be afraid, for God is close beside us . His rod and His staff protect and comfort us. Surely goodness and mercy shall follow You and I all the days of our lives. Let us live in Christ forever. He is the only one who can complete us. Thank you LORD for being true to your Word. Remember when you go through the valley, you are not standing still You are moving.

With Love and Adoration Mildred C Scales

Prayer List.

Prayer List.

Prayer List.

Prayer List.

Prayer List.

Prayer List.

Prayer List.

_____

_____

_____

_____

_____

_____

_____

_____

_____

_____

_____

_____

_____

_____

_____

_____

_____

_____

_____

_____

_____

Prayer List.

Scripture translations used

<u>New International Version. NIV</u>
<u>King James Version. KJV</u>
<u>New King James Version. NKJV</u>
<u>New living Translation. NLT</u>
<u>Willmington's Guide to the Bible</u>

A Prayer of Thanksgiving
Psalm 40:1,2

Psalm 40:7,8

When Praying Gods Protection
Psalm 139:6-10,14,18,23-24

Deuteronomy 31

Prayer of trust.
Lamentation 3:22-23

Psalm 3:3

James 5:16

Psalm 56:11

Comfort in the LORD.
Psalm 34:1-4,8,19

Deuteronomy 31:6

Philippians 4: 6-7

A Hunger for God.
Psalm 42: 1-2,7

Psalm 16:11

Psalm 8:4

www.ingramcontent.com/pod-product-compliance
Lightning Source LLC
Chambersburg PA
CBHW071323120626
46546CB00002B/418